In this series –

RUMI READINGS
FOR
SORROW & JOY

RUMI READINGS
FOR
SORROW & JOY

JALALUDDIN RUMI

The Scheherazade Foundation

The Scheherazade Foundation CIC
85 Great Portland Street
London
W1W 7LT
United Kingdom
www.SF.Charity
info@SF.Charity

First published by The Scheherazade Foundation CIC, 2025

RUMI READINGS FOR SORROW & JOY

A CIP catalogue record for this title is available from the British Library.

ISBN 978-1-915311-81-8

Introduction

Jalaluddin Rumi was born in Balkh, Afghanistan, in the year 1207, and died in Konya, Turkey, in 1273.

During the sixty-six years spanning this pair of dates, he produced a range of extraordinary work in Persian which, today, is classed as 'Sufi Mysticism'.

In the seven and a half centuries since his death, Rumi's corpus, which includes *The Masnavi* and *Fihi Ma Fihi*, has been circulated widely across the Near East, the Arab world, and Central Asia.

Generations of students continue to commit selections of the 60,000 verses to heart, and allow Rumi's way of thought to permeate through all areas of their lives.

Although Orientalists venturing eastward from Europe in the 1700s occasionally made note of Sufi Mysticism, they tended to witness it through the more theatrical frills – such as 'whirling dervishes' – rather than through a deep appreciation of the texts.

It wasn't until the close of the nineteenth century that the first wholescale translations of Rumi's written work began to appear in Europe.

Even then, they remained very much the purview of a few academics, whose translations were – even for the time – laden with indescribably floral and cumbersome prose.

Although in the Occident, students would find themselves scrutinizing Rumi's corpus, it wasn't until more recently that accessible appreciations of his work became available.

A few years before his death, I asked my father – the Sufi scholar and thinker Idries Shah – for his thoughts on Rumi's legacy in the West.

Sitting in his favourite chair, a porcelain cup of green tea in hand, he looked at me hard.

'I never cease to be amazed,' he said.

'Amazed by what?'

'By the way people don't take what's perfectly packaged, and ready and waiting for them, but rather obsess with something else.'

'With what?'

'With endless and nonsensical trimmings, trappings, and paraphernalia.'

My father sipped his tea.

After a moment of silent thought, he continued:

'Read Rumi in the original Persian,' he said, 'and so delicate are the verses that you have tears rolling down your cheeks. Yet here in the West, it's served up as something submerged in a thick, glutinous gravy, so much so that its utterly inedible.'

I reminded my father that a series of publications had recently found their way to press – publications that presented Rumi's couplets in an utterly new way.

Stripped bare of what my father had referred to as 'gravy', they were light.

Indeed, they were lighter than light.

My father rolled his eyes at the thought.

'In any other place, and at any other time,' he said, 'people would be up in arms. Or, if they weren't, they'd be laughing until their sides split. Imagine it – Western poets with absolutely no knowledge of the original Persian text touting new, bestselling editions of Rumi's work! It's what we call "The Soup of the Soup of the Soup".'

In the years since my father's death, Occidental society has been flooded with all things Rumi.

Couplets ascribed to him are read solemnly at weddings across the United States, Europe, and beyond.

Wisdom drawn from his poetry is tattooed daily over the backs and limbs of Hollywood A-listers.

But the precious words uttered at weddings, tattooed into skin, and quoted in abundance, hold little or no bearing to the original verses of Jalaluddin Rumi.

So, there it is…

The great Sufi Master's wisdom available:

(a) in a form that's unreadable because it's all covered in glutinous gravy, or

(b) in another form that's completely distorted – the Soup of the Soup of the Soup.

One thing that *is* evident is that the West can benefit enormously from a clean, clear rendition of Rumi's thinking – as the East has done over the last seven hundred years.

For this reason, we have commissioned entirely new translations, gleaned in particular from *The Masnavi*. Selected and translated by native Persian-speaking scholars, the emphasis has been on maintaining the lightness of Rumi's poetry.

In an age of relentless speed and digital overload, and so as to allow the work to be accessed by those who may benefit from it most, we have arranged a series of bite-sized morsels by way of theme.

We encourage you to do what students, scholars, and ordinary people have done across the East for centuries...

To pick a single couplet, or a handful – and to read them over and over, allowing them to seed themselves in your mind.

Little by little, having taken root, they will blossom and bear fruit.

Tahir Shah

How to Use This Book

Rumi Readings for Sorrow & Joy

This book holds a paradox:

That sorrow and joy are not enemies.

That they do not cancel each other out.

That they can – and often do – coexist in the same breath, the same moment, the same soul.

Rumi Readings for Sorrow & Joy gathers one hundred quotes drawn directly from *The Masnavi* and other classic works by the great Sufi master, freshly translated from the original Persian by The Scheherazade Foundation. These verses are presented not as mere reflections, but as **emotional companions** – ancient wisdom shaped into small, powerful mirrors.

The quotes are arranged in ten parts, guiding the reader through causes of sorrow, its forms and types, the nature of happiness, and the role of pain in personal transformation. You'll find expressions of grief, love, loneliness, delight, clarity, longing, and awakening – all treated with equal reverence.

This is not a book to make you feel only better.

It's a book to help you feel more fully.
And in that fullness, to come closer to truth.

Begin Where You Are

There is no set path through these pages.

You can start at the beginning. Or open anywhere. Let intuition or feeling guide you.

Sometimes you may seek joy and find sorrow.
Sometimes you may turn to sorrow and find joy.

This is the nature of life. This is the nature of the book.

Let it be what it is: a living text that changes with your mood, your season, your readiness.

Let the Quotes Open Something

After reading a quote – especially one that moves or unsettles you – take a moment to sit with it. Ask:

- What is this showing me about how I carry sorrow?
- What is this reminding me about how I welcome joy?

- What part of me wants to close… and what part is opening?

No need to answer fully. The point is not analysis. It's *awareness.*

If all you do is notice a shift inside you – a breath, a tear, a flicker – you're already doing the work.

Give Yourself Space

Sorrow and joy are both intense in their own ways.

Some quotes may land sharply. Some may feel almost too tender to touch. Others may bring sudden laughter, or peace.

Allow space for whatever arises.

You may wish to keep a journal of your responses. Ask questions. Let it prompt memories. Or just write what you're feeling, even if it has nothing to do with the quote.

For Those in Grief, For Those in Joy

This book meets you whether you are grieving or celebrating – and especially when you're somewhere in between.

In times of sorrow, these quotes can provide solace, witness, perspective.

In times of joy, they can bring grounding, gratitude, presence.

And in times of uncertainty – when you don't know what you're feeling, or why – they can offer quiet clarity.

Let them sit beside your emotions. Let them speak without fixing. Let them remain even when words fall short.

Share Gently

Some quotes may be perfect for sharing – at a celebration, in a condolence message, during a ritual, or in everyday moments when words are hard to find.

Share them gently. Let them carry meaning without the pressure of explanation.

Sometimes a single line is enough to honour a feeling – without trying to change it.

Let the Two Become One

Sorrow often teaches us things joy cannot.
And joy gives colour to the truths sorrow reveals.

Rumi knew this. He wrote not just as a mystic, but as a deeply feeling human being – someone who lost, who laughed, who burned with longing.

He invites us to hold sorrow and joy not as contradictions, but as companions.

He writes in this volume:
'The heart experiences both sorrow and laughter, being a place of paradox. A person who experiences both extremes is fully alive.'

Let this book accompany you through both.
Let it be a lantern – whether you're walking in brightness, or through the long night.

Part 1
Causes of Sorrow

1

The sorrows and troubles that burden our hearts
are like fleeting vapours
that emanate from our earthly existence.
As vapours vanish into the atmosphere,
these sorrows will eventually disappear,
leaving us with a clearer and lighter state of being.

2

Reckless and audacious behaviour
often invites misfortune and pain.
Those who breach the bonds of friendship
by acting thoughtlessly and carelessly
lose honour, and become like thieves
deserving no respect.

3

When you are busy with your own Self and desires,
you experience pain and suffering.
Yet when you detach from Self and embrace
an observing perspective,
you find peace and serenity.

4

When someone becomes overly sceptical
and refuses to believe anything
that they cannot see with their own eyes,
they may view even the vast universe as an insignificance.
In contrast, I find great peace and contentment
within myself,
because I choose to appreciate the beauty
and wonder of the world around me.
To me, this world is a Paradise
I am grateful to experience.

5

As sins accumulate,
the grip on your soul tightens,
causing anguish and distress.
After death, these bonds transform
into unbreakable chains.
Like a thief stealing gold,
the binding and sorrow consume the heart.
The individual wonders about the nature of this tightening,
which is actually the grip of the oppressed
crying out in agony.

6

The source of suffering has a discernible cause.
Divine retribution aligns suffering with wrongdoing.
God only punishes when He needs to.

7

In the human realm,
every desire, whether for material wealth,
the sustenance of life,
or even daily bread,
has the potential to exert
a powerful influence on our minds.
Like an intoxicating elixir,
these desires can captivate our thoughts and actions,
driving us to pursue them with unwavering determination.
But when our attempts to attain these desires fall short,
the resulting disappointment can strike us down,
leaving us dejected and disheartened.
This cycle of drunkenness and
sorrow becomes all-pervasive,
tainting and embittering experiences we once cherished.

8

A bird with clipped wings,
unable to soar,
left on the ground alone,
grieves and yearns.

9

People escape the suffering and misery
caused by their own excess and desires.
This suffering is a result of futile expectations,
which make people vulnerable to temptation.

10

When you forget to remember the one you love most,

pain and agony will seize you.

That was the discipline:

do not expect to be released from this eternal covenant.

Part 2

Factors
That Reduce Sorrow

11

In the intensity of a mystical state,
when a torrent of emotion surges wildly,
sorrows dissipate from consciousness.
As the torrent swells and finally overflows,
no vessel can contain its boundless force,
save for the very essence of water itself.

12

Overcoming suffering requires profound
connection with God.
To achieve true liberation,
you must cultivate deep understanding of the divine
and strive to embody generosity and forgiveness,
like Joseph of Canaan,[1]
who overcame adversity to achieve greatness.

---

1   Joseph of the multicoloured coat, as mentioned in Genesis.

13

Let us share in your sorrow, dear one.
Give us a taste of your grief to cleanse our souls.
When we drink from your sorrow,
it overwhelms us.
Grant us joy in place of sorrow and misery.

14

According to Luqman,[2]
patience is a virtue that serves as a shelter,
and a protective shield against the miseries of life.

---

2   Luqman the Wise, mentioned in the Qur'an.

15

When there is darkness,
light is no more.
And when the pure name of God is uttered,
all impurities and anxieties vanish.

16

Embracing love is the path to spiritual enlightenment, banishing suffering and granting entry to a higher realm.

17

Do not look for external solutions to your problems:
true healing and a cure come from within.

18

The heart experiences both sorrow and laughter,
being a place of paradox.
A person who experiences both extremes
is fully alive and lives the complete spectrum of feeling.
Love, vast and limitless,
brings forth both happiness and pain,
transcending the dualities of life.
Love remains constant and unwavering,
unaffected by changing seasons or happenstance.

19

Amidst grief and apprehension,
their sole focus is the pursuit of existence,
while, unknowingly, they drift towards extinction.

20

My heart is filled with sympathy for your sorrow,
even though I am a stranger to you.
Your grief comes to my heart like a dear friend,
for how else could my heart understand it?

Part 3

The Benefits of Sorrow

21

In times of hardship,
adversity serves as a wake-up call,
urging us to let go of our shortcomings
and strive for excellence.

22

Experience joy in your sorrows,
for they are the signs of reunion to come.
In this journey,
descent into the valleys is essential
for reaching higher peaks.
Your sorrow is like a treasure,
and your suffering a source of great discovery.
But only those who are truly wise and understanding
can enter this path.

23

During his lifetime,
he lived without difficulties
until he voiced his complaints to the wrathful Lord.
Even though God gave him the entire world
as his kingdom,
he was not protected from hidden pain and suffering.
But it was in this pain that he found solace,
for it gave him the opportunity to seek God's comfort
alone.

24

In times of adversity,
those who are struggling may lose their faith,
while those who are blessed may find their faith
strengthened.

25

When grief leaves the heart, or is endured,
it brings better things,
especially when you know for sure
that grief was the servant of the people of certainty.

26

Suffering and grief serve as a backdrop to happiness, strengthening its value and making it more distinct.

27

In the embrace of pain
resides mercy;
freshness blossoms when barriers are broken.
In times of darkness and cold winds,
patience bursts forth in the heart of those who are broken.
The elixir of life,
the cup of ecstasy:
these treasures lie hidden in the depths of adversity.

28

Acknowledge and accept sadness
and fear as natural parts of life.
Find meaning and purpose in death.
Resist the cravings and desires of the Self,
which lead to disappointment and suffering.

29

In the darkness of night,
a treasure of mercy is unveiled,
granting brief respite from worldly desire.
When faced with limitation,
O traveller,
recognize that it is for your own benefit,
and resist the temptation to become consuming fire.
Within the cycles of constriction and expansion,
there lies abundance of opportunity
for boundless growth and fulfilment.

30

If God wants to support us,
He makes us pray.
Every time you weep,
eventually there will be joy.
A servant who can foresee the outcome is blessed:
mercy triumphs wherever there are tears.

Part 4

The Forms
of Worldly Grief

31

His authority is over demons, not angels.
Suffering exists on earth,
not in heaven.
Stop striving to be loved and instead become a lover.
O deceived one, you assume you are good,
but this is not true.

32

Cheerful children and exhausted adults:
illness from anger,
and happiness as a tonic for the heart.

33

I am filled with joy:
I have no sorrows or anxieties.
What could possibly disturb me?
The bitterness of the world does not affect me at all.

34

In the darkness, an army of sorrow arises,
but victory belongs to the joy of the wise.
With your beauty,
enhance the happiness of the joyful even more.
Let sorrow and grief remain within themselves.

35

Sorrow causes all to mourn,
uniting the men and women of Afghanistan.
This pain has become an overpowering oppressor,
formidable and unrelenting like a dragon.

36

Sorrow, depart from this place,
or else be prepared to endure
the repercussions of your presence.
The darkness of the night cannot overshadow
the brilliance of the moon.

37

O sorrow,

if you turn into something cherished by my beloved,

then you are not a burden to me.

When one is truly devoted and finds sweetness in love,

there is no need to deny the anguish and struggle

it may entail.

Despite sorrow's cruelty,

ruthlessness and unpleasantness,

my heart still yearns for the pure and virtuous beloved.

Our ultimate goal remains unchanged:

to reach and be with them.

38

Embrace the vastness
and depths of the sea without fear.
Trust in the call to fearlessness,
for it holds the answer.
When God grants you the decree of fearlessness,
He provides abundant nourishment,
just as the sea sustains life.
True fear is the absence of fear,
not its presence.
In this state of fearlessness,
there is no sorrow, only joy and happiness.

39

In the midst of life's chaotic battles,
you lose sight of your true Self,
mistaking multiple identities for your essence.
You claim ownership of different forms, declaring,
'This is who I am.'
When, in reality,
you are constantly changing and evolving.
Despite being surrounded by others,
you feel alone, consumed by sorrow and contemplation.

40

In the grip of sadness and despair,

we weep,

feeling isolated and immersed in a sea of misery.

Our eyes, filled with tears,

could form whole rivers and streams.

There exists a kind of suffering more painful than death,

one to which there is no remedy, no solution.

In light of this,

how can anyone possibly suggest

that this anguish can be cured or alleviated?

Part 5
Types of Sorrow

41

The intellect is unaware of certain profound thoughts;
it only bears the weight of God's sorrow.
Choose the path of religious devotion:
God will alleviate all other sorrows.

42

Within every community
people find their kin and forge bonds.
I belong to my own people and lineage;
our love is intertwined with sadness.

43

Like autumn's adieu,
my heart aches with sorrow of separation,
casting a darkening hue over the garden of my soul.
When will your presence,
like that of a beautiful spring,
arrive to unveil the hidden splendour within my heart?

44

Love, though it may come from beyond,
penetrates deeply into the heart already filled
with sadness.

45

Why linger in this unfamiliar land, my beloved?
Return to your roots and cease your self-inflicted suffering.
None in this dismal abode recognize your worth.
Do not tarry among these callous souls:
you are a priceless gem.
Come back home.

46

Only a cold-hearted person,
incapable of perceiving beauty,
can see you and not lose themselves.
Such insensitivity makes them immune
to all other calamities in life.

47

Our bond is like that between a fish and the sea;
I am deeply connected to you and cherish you.
Have mercy on me, my King,
because without you
I am lost and alone.
A world without you cannot be borne.
May I always be with you,
for with you,
I find life and meaning;
without you,
all is chaos and pain.

48

Comfort the afflicted,
as you yourself need comfort.
Do not dwell on their sins or reject them,
for they are already burdened by adversity.
May those who offer kindness and compassion
extend their support to ease their suffering.

49

Without you,
my beloved,
patience eludes me.
O soul of purity,
the source of generosity and faithfulness,
reveal yourself to me!
Patience finds no refuge
when Mount Qaf,[3]
immense in its steadfastness,
dissolves like snow
under the relentless sun of separation.

---

3   A mythological mountain.

50

Tonight, solitude weighs heavy on my heart;
I long for your presence
to share the depths of my emotions with you.
My soul is like a reed flute,
echoing with lamentations and woes
which I hope will reach you
as a sweet and poignant melody.
No longer am I merely a vessel of breath;
these laments now serve
as a vessel of enlightenment from my heart.

Part 6

The Causes of Happiness

51

Love is the source of all happiness,
and lovers come to life through its radiance.
Love reigns supreme,
and lovers prosper under its rule and colours.

52

O heart,
you have been captivated by love,
and you are fortunate
to have discovered such valuable treasure.
You have transcended the boundaries of space and time,
and your realm has been blessed with prosperity.
Your once-uncertain doubts have transformed
into unwavering belief,
erasing any trace of bitterness.
You have become an enchanting delicacy,
a feast for the senses,
with an abundance of sweetness
that brings delight to all who encounter it.

53

Let us immerse ourselves in pure joy
and cast away all remnants of sorrow
and distress.

54

O union,
you are the source of joy
with your diverse forms,
and profound significance bringing immense delight.

55

Amidst the vastness of the world and life's intricacies,
find amusement and laughter within your own being.
Every physical attribute,
both perfect and imperfect,
holds a humorous charm
that deserves acknowledgment.

56

Your mental disposition determines your surroundings.
If you focus on beauty and positivity,
you will find yourself surrounded by beautiful things.
But if you focus on negativity and bitterness,
you will find yourself surrounded by unpleasantness.

57

Suffering stems from desiring things
that cannot be obtained.
When we no longer desire those unattainable things,
suffering disappears of its own accord.

58

Embrace universal love,
and create a garden of vibrant flowers
within your heart.
Let your essence be like an orchard in bloom,
filling every space with beauty and perfume.
Wherever you gaze,
may you see the green landscape surrounding your soul.
May each glance bring visions of bright blossoms
and captivating scent.

59

The Almighty created humans in two forms:
some are steadfast and stable like the earth,
bearing numerous burdens,
while others are dynamic and fluid like water.
When these two beings interact,
a beautiful transformation occurs.
The flowing water nourishes the earth,
giving rise to rose gardens, lush trees, and bountiful fruits.
These natural wonders provide
sustenance and strength to souls,
symbolizing the eternal bond
between the steadfast and dynamic aspects of creation.

60

The existence of another world
is marked by the continuous cycle
of new beginnings and endings.
Each day, night, garden, and snare are new,
and every breath brings fresh thoughts,
happiness, and riches.
But where does the new originate,
and where does the old vanish to?
If the world extends beyond what we perceive,
it is boundless like a flowing stream
that appears confined yet keeps moving.
The emergence of new elements and the passing of old ones
raises questions about the source of this endless cycle.

Part 7

How to Live Happily

61

O God,
let Your mercy be upon me;
replace my torn clothes with Your garment of grace.
Your kindness overwhelms me:
shatter my confusion with Your blessings.
If the world is destined for sorrow,
then let me share in that sorrow and sadness.

62

I advised not to associate with those
bearing sadness and sorrow,
but to seek out the company of those
who bring joy and serenity.
I urged you to avoid troubles and difficulties,
and to be surrounded by beauty and pleasant things.

63

Seek a companion to confide in:
sharing your sorrows can ease the pain within.
Like a flower that eagerly blooms,
its beauty and fragrance remain concealed.

64

Remain quiet, as the stillness of the ocean;
do not talk excessively, like a stream.
The ocean,
in all its quietude,
will then come to you,
rather than your rushing toward the stream,
and its needless conversation.

65

Truly blessed is the person
who, in their youth,
saw wisdom in seizing opportunities,
and promptly repaid their debts
when strength, health, courage, and vigour flourished.
They willingly embraced the challenges of life
while their youth still bloomed,
like a lush and fertile garden offering blessings.

66

Despite apparent emptiness,
there is much to discover and appreciate with our eyes.
Even in moments of despair,
there is hope and potential for joy.

67

The judge says
that we should be satisfied with our lives,
because every challenge and difficulty is a part of destiny.
He is content with his fate,
even if sometimes it leads to pain.
He compares his heart to a garden,
where inner joy and peace
allow him to find happiness
even in the most difficult of times.

68

In this world
there is no joy that lasts:
all fades, like a shadow passing.
Remember, others have felt this delight;
yet it vanished, leaving them in darkness.
Hold on to nothing,
let your heart be free
before the world takes its joy from you.

69

Happiness comes from within,
not from possessions,
or grand palaces and castles.
Some people may find joy and fulfilment in simple,
humble spaces like the corner of a mosque,
while others may seek it in elaborate gardens,
but remain dissatisfied.
True joy is found through internal peace and contentment,
not externals and circumstance.

70

Your upbringing guides your thoughts,
as thoughtful deliberation avoids mistakes.
Just like a river's continuous flow,
it stays pure and clear without any hindrance.
This deliberation brings prosperity and joy.
It is like an egg hatching into wealth,
or birds flying free to find fortune.

Part 8

Dimensions & Characteristics of Happiness

71

The sun's brilliance stems from a tiny particle,
while Venus, like a chalice,
yearns to be filled.
Similarly, a soul lacking its intrinsic essence is ensnared,
much like the sun constrained by life's complexities:
a poignant image of confinement.

72

The physical body often serves as an obstacle,
diverting attention away from the soul.

73

The prophets achieved genuine joy and satisfaction
by drawing from the wellspring of authentic happiness,
namely, Truth.
Having tasted this,
worldly pleasures and possessions
appeared trivial and meaningless:
an experience like finding a living,
vibrant entity that captivates your whole attention.
How, then, can you embrace a lifeless and mundane
existence devoid of all vitality?

74

Those who overcome the allure of fleeting pleasures discover enduring contentment from within.

75

In the realm of life,
those who endure the trials and tribulations of adversity
in the prison of affliction are often rewarded
with meagre sustenance and fleeting pleasures.
While those who bask in the glory of fortune
within the confines of a palace
face the relentless struggle of battle,
and the weight of hardship as their recompense.

76

The pursuit of desires is deceptive and fleeting,
like a dark illusion surrounding a brief glimmer of light.
This light of temptation and metaphor,
like a spark, dances in the shadows,
leading you down a long and winding path.
Your words and actions are ignored
and your journey remains uncharted.
You stumble, sometimes falling into the depths,
sometimes grazing the surface,
all the while unaware of your true destination.

77

As life progresses and the physical aspects
of our existence diminish,
the inner glow and spiritual light of the soul grow
and shine more brightly.
The fading of earthly pleasures allows for an illumination
of the soul's radiance.

78

Despite flying high,
the bird cannot escape its own shadow.
And when it is on the ground,
the shadow remains.
The unwise hunter pursued this shadow
because he lacked knowledge of its reality.
The more he followed, the farther it seemed to move;
he never realized it was a mere shade,
not the bird itself.

79

A man had a donkey but no saddle.
When he got a saddle,
a wolf snatched the donkey.
He then got a jug,
but he couldn't cup his hand to catch the water.
When he finally found some water,
he dropped the jug, and it broke.

80

When desires of the Self
and illusions overwhelm the soul,
the mind mourns,
while the Self rejoices.

Part 9

Qualities
of True Happiness

81

When you receive divine spiritual inspiration,
and your heart expands with love and compassion,
that spiritual essence does not become separate from you.
Similarly, when you embody truthfulness and integrity,
others do not experience
that truthfulness separately from you.

82

In my freedom from worldly pleasures,
I find true happiness.
Without the influence of wine,
I feel a natural state of joy.
I am self-sufficient and content,
not reliant on external factors for my well-being.
May this inner fulfilment be recognized
and cherished.

83

Despite its sorrowful state,
the laughing flower cannot cry.
Instead, it brings joy to others by inspiring lilies
and roses to bloom in the speaker's heart.

84

Wisdom's joy endures;
worldly pleasures do not.

85

Every beautiful melody
originated from the celestial realm.
The music of flutes and drums
echoes the melodies played by Israfil.[4]
Music originated from the movement
of the celestial spheres.
Before arriving on Earth,
we resided in Paradise,
and were familiar with heavenly harmonies.
The echoes of truth whisper in our ears as we listen.

---

4   An archangel in Islamic tradition, often associated with Raphael.

86

Joining our Sultan as a servant
will bring you happiness and joy,
even during times of universal sorrow and grief.

87

Our happiness and joy are beyond measure,
because you have graced us
with your captivating presence.

88

Companionship nourishes the heart,
and knowledge purifies it.
Just as rain nourishes the soil,
producing fruits, flowers and fragrances,
human interaction brings joy, contentment, and
cheerfulness.
When cheerfulness touches the soul
it fosters generosity and kindness.

89

Those who embrace genuine happiness
become embodiments of joy,
radiating warmth
and spreading cheer like a benevolent sun.
Their presence exudes positivity,
inviting others to partake
in the delightful celebration of shared happiness.

90

Everyone experiences
both joy and sorrow in their lives.
These joys and sorrows
influence the existence and demise of
different parts of the body
and aspects of life:
pregnancy comes from desire
and the enjoyment of physical intimacy;
a garden in bloom
comes from the arrival of spring.
The interaction between elements
is essential for creation and sustenance.

Part 10

The Role of Pain
in Joy & Sorrow

91

In times of spiritual doubt and emotional pain
caused by wrongdoing,
superficial identity and illusory existence are challenged:
a recognition prompting profound awakening,
shedding the cloak of Self and unveiling the path
towards Truth and unity.

92

A person tormented
by the sun experiences unending agony,
a perpetual state of hopelessness and anguish.

93

When arrogance fills your mind,
and you feel superior to others,
tread cautiously.
Those who challenge your pride
will become your enemies,
and animosity will arise within you.
You will harbour grudges against them.

94

When life's challenges
make the world constrict around you,
God transforms the bitterness of suffering into sweetness.
He encourages patience and whispers:
'Yes, my pure one, listen, endure, and be patient.
As dawn approaches,
remain composed and do not speak too much.
I am working for your benefit,
so trust in my plan, and find solace.'

95

Despite being blessed with grace and exceptional talent,
I am left with nothing tangible to show for it
except for fanciful dreams
that have no foundation in reality,
and the challenges that come with such qualities.

96

In plaintive tones,
the reed flute weaves a narrative
filled with sorrow,
mourning the separations it has endured.
Ever since it was taken from its humble home,
the reed bed, its lamenting melodies have stirred emotions,
evoking feelings of grief and longing
in the hearts of countless listeners.

97

When judgement lies in the hands of rogues,
they inevitably murder a mystic like Mansur al-Hallaj.[5]
When the power is in the hands of the ignorant,
fools kill prophets.

---

5   Executed in 922 C.E.

98

God sends trials and hardships to strengthen the soul.
Just as a coin is created
through the process of heating and striking,
so, too, do challenges forge the spirit within.
These trials, such as cold, suffering, scarcity, and fear,
serve to reveal the true worth and resilience of the soul.

99

Embracing detachment from desires and Self,
which represents the stage of poverty,
will safeguard your soul and spirit from destruction.
Your soul, like a garden,
will bloom and become beautiful.
You will find tranquility where others find dread,
like a seagull finding strength in the mighty roar of the sea,
in contrast to a timid, domesticated bird.

100

Emotional suffering from separation and reunion
is not inherent,
but a result of our attachments and self-centredness.
Focusing on these superficial aspects
blinds us to the true nature of reality,
which remains unaffected by our personal experiences.

Finis

www.ingramcontent.com/pod-product-compliance
Lightning Source LLC
Chambersburg PA
CBHW020451100426
42813CB00031B/3326/J